Copyright © 2021 by Ruben Hammond -All rights reserved.

No part of this publication may be reproduced, distributed, or transmitted in any form or by any means, including photocopying, recording, or other electronic or mechanical methods, without the prior written permission of the publisher, except in the case of brief quotations embodied in reviews and certain other non-commercial uses permitted by copyright law.

This Book is provided with the sole purpose of providing relevant information on a specific topic for which every reasonable effort has been made to ensure that it is both accurate and reasonable. Nevertheless, by purchasing this Book you consent to the fact that the author, as well as the publisher, are in no way experts on the topics contained herein, regardless of any claims as such that may be made within. It is recommended that you always consult a professional prior to undertaking any of the advice or techniques discussed within.This is a legally binding declaration that is considered both valid and fair by both the Committee of Publishers Association and the American Bar Association and should be considered as legally binding within the United States.

CONTENTS

INTRODUCTION

The Ninja Foodi Digital Air Fryer Oven is essentially a smart and extremely versatile cooking appliance that has revolutionized how we cook and prepare meals!

This particular cooking appliance is one of the first of its kind from Ninja Kitchen. It has some excellent features not found on any other Air Fryer ovens.

Once you unbox the appliance,e you will find the rectangular unit, which contains a flip lid and control panel on the front. The Air Fryer basket, sheet pan, crumb tray are also provided and are removable.

The crumb tray is placed inside and at the Oven's bottom to prevent the food drippings from falling on the oven base. The sheet pan is used for baking, broiling, or toasting. Whereas the Air fryer basket is used to evenly air fry the food. The wire rack can also be used for roasting purposes.

The incredible benefits of Ninja Foodi Pro Air Fryer Oven

Air Fryers these days are gaining much popularity, thanks to their promise of delivering exceptionally tasty "Fried" food that requires minimal oil or fat to prepare.

While they are really good, versatile appliances such as the Ninja Foodi Pro Air Fryer Oven are effortlessly taking the ball out of their court, with their wide array of functionalities and brilliant form factors.

Appliances such as these are combined with the powers of an Air Fryer and Counter-top ovens to save up more space and provide an amazing alternative to having multiple appliances in the kitchen, each for a specific job.

Sure, these Air Fryer Oven's fall themselves fall on a bulkier side, especially when compared to smaller sized Air Fryers or Toaster Ovens. But if you look at the big picture and assess just how many functions they pack under their hood, space doesn't really feel like a big deal.

The Ninja® Foodi™ Digital Air Fry Oven gives you the best of both worlds.

It provides lots of space to cook for your family and flips up and away when not in use. It has a re movable crumb tray and an accessible back panel for easy, thorough cleaning. With a range of co oking functions and temperatures, it can handle everything from breakfast bagels to french fries, to a family-size sheet pan meal, to a delicate dessert.

Convenience in storage

While the appliance's cooking surface is family size, it really won't take over your whole kitchen counter. That''s because while you are not using the appliance, you will have the option to easily flip it up, which saves almost 50 percent space as opposed to when keeping it folded. The sleek design ensures that it looks stylish and awesome in your kitchen no matter how you keep it.

Simple and efficient cleaning

Both the sheet pan and Air Fryer basket and extremely easy to clean and dishwasher safe. As for the Oven, you can simply wipe it with a damp cloth to clean it up. The crumb tray slides out very easily, and the back of the Oven opens up as well, giving you full access to the interior from both the front and the back.

Large cooking area

The square sheet pan and the air fry basket measure approximately 13 by 13 inches. That's about one-and-a-half times the size of some small toaster ovens. You can easily cook a full meal for four or party food for a crowd without cooking multiple batches. The sheet pan can hold nine slices of bread at once. Nine!

Reduce cook times

Regardless of your mode, whether Air Fry, Broil, or Roast, the Ninja Foodi Digital Air Fry Oven will cook faster than traditional toaster ovens / Air Fryers. The convention fan here speeds up the cooking by almost 60%, making sure that you can make your weekend delights in a jiffy! Spend less time in the kitchen and more time with your family.

Even and efficient heating

The Ninja Foodi Digital Air Fry Oven preheats in about 60 seconds. Compare that with the 10 to 15 minutes, a conventional oven takes to heat up, or even the five minutes a small toaster oven or air fryer takes. You'll start to see how fast you can have dinner on the table.

Toasting Function

This is possibly one of the very few Oven out in the market that can work like a toaster! On the control panel, you will find 2 options for toasting (bread and bagel): you will select "bagel" if you want to toast some bagels or simply "toast" if you want to toast some bread slices. You will be able to fit and toast up to 9 slices of bread at a time; in this way, no one will be waiting for their toasts to be done.

Press the "time/slice" button and then turn the dial to choose the number of slices you would like to toast. Press the "temp/darkness" button and choose the level of darkness/lightness for your bread slices. You can get crispy dark brown, golden brown, or even soft light brown toasts as you desire.

Healthier Meals

With the Air Frying function, you will get your food with 75% less fat than traditional frying methods. This has been tested either for hand-cut and deep-fried French fries.

Extremely User Friendly And Efficient

All the features, including the control panel, are very easy to understand and to use. All buttons are cleared marked for each and single function. The main dial will allow you to switch from one mode to another and decrease or increase the cooking time. You can press this same dial for pausing or starting a function. Moreover, the display will also appear when the device has to complete the cooling down procedure. The Oven is ready to be flipped up.

Understanding the functions of the Oven

Despite having a wide array of features under its belt, using the Ninja Foodi Digital Air Fry Oven is possibly easier to learn. Just one dial controls the whole cooking process, making everything a very seamless experience.

All you have to do is select the cooking function, set the timer, the temperature, and initiate the cooking process; that's it! The appliance will always automatically stop whenever you might need to add an ingredient or give the ingredient a stir.

The Oven can switch between Fahrenheit and Celsius temperature units. It will even let you know it's preheating or when it is cool enough to clean/flip for storage.

Everything about this appliance has been designed with usability and accessibility in mind. Each aspect of the Oven is crafted to be as simple and easy to read and use as possible.

The most important area of the Oven where you will find all the functions is the control panel.

On the control panel, you'll see the time and temperature display. You'll see the number of slices and darkness level in the Toast or Bagel modes instead of time and temperature. Icons indicate when the unit is preheating, when it is hot and whether the Oven is set to Fahrenheit or Celsius. The selected function lights up under Crisp Control when the Oven is turned on. The time display reads FLIP when the unit is cool enough to flip up for storage.

Under the function settings is the multifunctional dial. It starts and pauses the Oven and adjusts the time and temperature (or several slices and darkness level for toast). The Time button starts and completes setting the time (or several toast slices). The Temperature button does the same for temperature (or darkness level for toast). The oven light and OFF/ON button are at the bottom of the control panel.

With that, let me discuss the core functions of the Oven in brief details for you to easily understand and use them properly:

Air Fry

The Air Frye mode is possibly the most used setting that mimics an Air Fryer's cooking function. This mode will give you an excellent and crispy exterior with a fully cooked interior.

Bagel

The Bagel setting uses no fan and provides slightly lower heat from the top rather from the bottom. The Ninja Foodi Digital Air Fry Oven will toast about 6 bagel slices at a time. Like the toast feature, this mode has no temperature setting, as the temperature is adjusted according to the number of slices inside the appliance.

Toast

Like the bagel function, the toast function uses no fan and even heat from both the top and bottom elements. The Ninja Foodi Digital Air Fry Oven can toast a maximum of 9 slices of bread in one batch. The number of slices determines the timer, temperature automatically. You just need to tell the appliance if you want light or dark toast, and the Oven will take care of the rest.

Bake

The baking setting again uses no heat from the fan but uses the top and bottom heating elements to produce the heat required. The timer can be set up to 2 hours. The temperature can be adjusted within a range of 250 degrees F and 450 degrees F. This setting is awesome for delicate dishes and desserts. It is awesome for warming tortillas as well.

Air Broil

The Air Broil setting uses medium convection fan speed and high heat from the top element. The time can be set up to 30 minutes and the temperature set to HIGH or LOW. It's useful for browning chops, steaks, or chicken or fish fillets.

Air Roast

The Air Roast feature is best for sheet pan recipes and for roasting meals. It uses medium convection fan speed and even heats from the top and bottom elements. The timer can be set to 2 hours, and the temperature can be adjusted from a range of 250 degrees F to 450 degrees F.

The necessary steps of using the Oven

You should know that the process for using Air Fry, Air Roast, Air Broil, and Bake are pretty much the same, so I will break them down first.

- To start up the cooking process, first, you have to select the function that you need.
- The default time and temperature setting will display; you should know that the Oven will also remember your last t/me and temperature used, which is an excellent feature if you repeat recipes from time to time
- To adjust the time, press the Time/Slice button and use the dial to change the timer. Press the button again to set it.
- To set the temperature, press the Temp/Darkness button and turn the dial; press the button again to set it.
- Once done, place the food on your Air Fry basket or sheet pan as needed; Press Start/Pause to begin cooking.

Now, for the toast and bagel functions:

- To start the toasting process, use the dial to select the function that you need
- The default number of slices and darkness level will be shown; just like the other functions, the Oven will remember your most recently used feature
- Place bread/bagels, cut side-up on the rack
- Adjust the number of slices, press the Time/Slice button, and use the dial to change it
- Press the Time/Slice button again to set the number of slices
- Adjust how dark you want your toast/bagels to beby pressing the Temp/Darkness button and setting the dial to your desired level
- Press the button again to fix it
- Press the Start/Pause button to start it

Essential accessories to have

Another advantage to cooking with the Ninja® Foodi™ Digital Air Fry Oven is that you won't need a cabinet full of equipment. For most of the recipes, you'll only need the sheet pan once you start cooking. A couple of the recipes use the Air Fry basket, and some of the Staples recipes use a baking pan. But that's it—no pots and pans, no skillets. You may want to order a second sheet pan from Ninja so you'll have a backup, but that's optional.

Timer: I find that an extra timer helps when I have to check a dish halfway through to turn or toss ingredients. That way, I can set the Ninja Foodi Digital Air Fry Oven for the total time and not reset it.

Meat thermometer: When you start using a new appliance, you may find that your usual recipes don't cook at the same rate. It's best to be safe when cooking chicken thighs or pork chops and checking their internal temperature during cooking.

Oil mister/sprayer: I call for cooking oil spray in some recipes, and while you can use a store-bought spray, I know that some cooks prefer to use their own oil in a spray bottle.

Prep tools: For prep, you'll need a cutting board and knives, and a few bowls—small ones for sauces, larger ones for mixing ingredients. Other necessary tools include whisks and spoons for stirring and spatulas and tongs for moving food around. Of course, you'll need sturdy, thick pot holders or oven mitts for getting the hot sheet pan out of the Oven.

CHAPTER 1: BREAKFAST

Juicy Ratatouille

(Prepping time: 10 minutes \ Cooking time: 10-30 minutes |For 4 servings)

Ingredients

- ½ cup zucchini
- 1 yellow pepper
- 2 tomatoes
- 1 onion, peeled
- 1 garlic clove, crushed
- 2 teaspoons dried herbs
- Fresh ground black pepper
- 1 tablespoon olive oil

Directions

1. Arrange drip pan in the bottom of the Air Fryer Oven cooking chamber
2. Preheat your Air Fryer to 392 degrees F in "AIR FRY" mode
3. Cut zucchini, bell pepper, tomatoes, and onion into small cubes
4. Take a bowl and mix in garlic, herbs, ½ teaspoon salt, season with pepper, stir in olive oil
5. Place bowl in basket and slide into Air Fryer
6. Cook for 15 minutes, stir vegetables once when the "Turn Food" mode shows

Stir well and enjoy it!

Nutrition Values (Per Serving)

- Calories: 421
- Fat: 24g
- Carbohydrates: 10g
- Protein: 10g
- Sodium: 880g
- Fiber: 2g
- Saturated Fat: 2g

Bacon-Wrapped Asparagus Meal

(Prepping time: 10 minutes \ Cooking time: 20 minutes |For 4 servings)

Ingredients

- 1 bunch of asparagus
- 4 slices streaky bacon
- 1 tablespoon brown sugar
- 1 and ½ tablespoons olive oil
- 1 teaspoon brown sugar
- Garlic pepper seasoning

Directions

1. Arrange drip pan in the bottom of the Air Fryer Oven cooking chamber
2. Preheat your air fryer to 400 degrees F for 8 minutes in "AIR FRY" mode
3. Trim the asparagus to your desired length
4. Take a bowl and add oil, garlic pepper, sugar to make a mixture
5. Coat the asparagus with the mix
6. Wrap one piece of bacon with an asparagus stalk
7. To secure the wrap, poke a toothpick
8. Place all the wraps in the basket in your Vortex Air Fryer
9. Cook for 8 minutes
10. Serve and enjoy!

Nutrition Values (Per Serving)

- Calories: 178
- Fat: 25g
- Carbohydrates: 10g
- Protein: 48g
- Sodium: 506 g
- Fiber: 2g
- Saturated Fat: 9g

Feisty Cup-A-Ham

(Prepping time: 10 minutes \ Cooking time: 4 minutes |For 4 servings)

Ingredients

- 2 cups cream cheese
- 2 eggs
- 1 pack stevia
- ½ teaspoon Cinnamon

Directions

1. Arrange drip pan in the bottom of the Air Fryer Oven cooking chamber
2. Preheat your Air Fryer Oven to 330 degrees F in "AIR FRY" mode
3. Place the eggs and stevia in a bowl
4. Whisk until stevia is dissolved
5. Add the cream cheese and cinnamon to eggs
6. Whisk until smooth
7. Ladle the quarter of the batter into the air fryer
8. Cook for 2 minutes at 330 degrees F
9. Flip the pancake and then cook for 2 minutes more
10. Repeat the process
11. Serve and enjoy!

Nutrition Values (Per Serving)

- Calories: 329
- Fat: 30g
- Carbohydrates: 6g
- Protein: 310g
- Sodium: 813g
- Fiber: 2g
- Saturated Fat: 8g

Perfect Baked Veggie Quiche

(Prepping time: 10 minutes\ Cooking time: 30 minutes |For 2 servings)

Ingredients

- 2 cups spinach, chopped
- 1 bell pepper, chopped
- 1 cup mushrooms, sliced
- 1 teaspoon olive oil
- 2 cups liquid egg substitute
- 4 ounces mozzarella cheese, shredded
- ½ teaspoon garlic powder
- ½ teaspoon onion powder
- Salt and pepper

Directions

1. Place your pan over medium heat and add oil
2. Heat the oil
3. Add mushrooms and bell pepper into your pan
4. Sauté until it becomes tender
5. Remove the pan from heat
6. Let it cool
7. Take a bowl and add egg substitute, spinach, cheese, onion powder, garlic powder, salt and pepper
8. Stir in mushrooms and bell pepper
9. Pour into the greased muffin pan
10. Place the wire rack on Level 2
11. Preheat by pressing the "BAKE" option and setting it to 350 degrees F
12. Set the timer to 30 minutes
13. Let it preheat until you hear a beep
14. Place the baking dish on a wire rack and close the oven door
15. Cook for 30 minutes
16. Serve and enjoy!

Nutrition Values (Per Serving)

- Calories: 330
- Fat: 10.4 g
- Saturated Fat: 3 g
- Carbohydrates: 11.4 g
- Fiber: 3 g
- Sodium: 690 mg
- Protein: 48 g

Spinach Feta Frittata

(Prepping time: 10 minutes\ Cooking time: 30 minutes |For 2 servings)

Ingredients

- 3 ounces fresh spinach, chopped
- 2 ounces scallions, chopped
- 6 eggs
- 5 ounces mushrooms, sliced
- 2 tablespoons olive oil
- 4 ounces feta cheese, crumbled
- Salt and pepper

Directions

1. Take a large bowl and add whisked eggs, cheese, salt, and pepper
2. Place a pan over medium heat and add oil
3. Add scallions and mushrooms, sauté for 10 minutes
4. Add spinach and sauté for 2 minutes
5. Pour egg mixture into your greased baking dish
6. Place the wire rack on Level 2
7. Preheat by pressing the "BAKE" option and setting it to 350 degrees F
8. Set the timer to 20 minutes
9. Let it preheat until you hear a beep
10. Place the baking dish on a wire rack and close the oven door
11. Cook for 20 minutes
12. Serve and enjoy!

Nutrition Values (Per Serving)

- Calories: 575
- Fat: 48 g
- Saturated Fat: 9 g
- Carbohydrates: 9 g
- Fiber: 3 g
- Sodium: 494 mg
- Protein: 29 g

Mushroom Zucchini Frittata

(Prepping time: 10 minutes\ Cooking time: 20 minutes |For 2 servings)

Ingredients

- 1 cup zucchini, chopped
- 4 eggs
- 1 cup cheddar cheese
- 1 tablespoon olive oil
- 1 cup mushrooms, sliced
- 1 cup bell peppers, chopped ½ cup onion, chopped
- 2 tablespoons milk
- Salt and pepper

Directions

1. Place a pan over medium heat and add oil into it
2. Add zucchini, onion, bell pepper, and mushrooms
3. Sauté for 5 minutes
4. Remove the pan and let it cool
5. Take a bowl and whisk the egg with milk, salt, and pepper
6. Add sautéed vegetables and cheese
7. Stir them well
8. Pour egg mixture into the greased baking dish
9. Place the wire rack on Level 2
10. Preheat by pressing the "BAKE" option and setting it to 350 degrees F
11. Set the timer to 20 minutes
12. Let it preheat until you hear a beep
13. Place the baking dish on a wire rack and close the oven door
14. Cook for 20 minutes
15. Serve and enjoy!

Nutrition Values (Per Serving)

- Calories: 566
- Fat: 46 g
- Saturated Fat: 10 g
- Carbohydrates: 11 g
- Fiber: 3 g
- Sodium: 245 mg
- Protein: 32 g

Cool Mushroom Quiche

(Prepping time: 10 minutes\ Cooking time: 40 minutes |For 6 servings)

Ingredients

- 10 ounces spinach, frozen, thawed, and drained
- 1 cup mozzarella cheese, shredded
- 2 cheese slices, cut into pieces
- 6 eggs
- 8 ounces can mushroom, sliced
- 1/3 cup parmesan cheese, shredded
- ½ cup heavy cream
- ½ cup of water
- ½ teaspoon garlic powder
- Salt and pepper

Directions

1. Take a baking dish and spread mushroom and spinach
2. Arrange cheese on top
3. Take a bowl and add garlic powder, parmesan cheese, whisked egg with heavy cream, water, salt, and pepper
4. Pour the egg mixture over mushroom and spinach
5. Top them with mozzarella cheese
6. Place the wire rack on Level 2
7. Preheat by pressing the "BAKE" option and setting it to 350-degree F
8. Set the timer to 40 minutes
9. Let it preheat until you hear a beep
10. Place the baking dish on a wire rack and close the oven door
11. Cook for 40 minutes
12. Serve and enjoy!

Nutrition Values (Per Serving)

- Calories: 185
- Fat: 13 g
- Saturated Fat: 3 g
- Carbohydrates: 5 g
- Fiber: 2 g
- Sodium: 345 mg
- Protein: 13 g

Early Morning Bacon Omelet

(Prepping time: 5-10 minutes\ Cooking time: 10 minutes| For 4 servings)

Ingredients

- 4 whole eggs, whisked
- 4 tomatoes, cubed
- 1 tablespoon olive oil
- 1 tablespoon cheddar, grated
- 1 tablespoon parsley, chopped
- ¼ pound cubed, cooked, and chopped
- Salt and pepper, to taste

Directions

1. Add bacon into a small-sized pan
2. Heat the pan over medium heat
3. Sauté for 2 minutes
4. Add bacon with remaining ingredients into a bowl
5. Stir well and sprinkle cheese on top
6. Preheat your Air Fryer Oven Pro by pressing the "BAKE" mode at 400 degrees F temperature
7. Set the timer to 10 minutes
8. Pour the mixture into a baking dish
9. Transfer it to your Ninja Foodi Smart XL Grill
10. Bake for 8 minutes
11. Serve and enjoy!

Nutrition Values (Per Serving)

- Calories: 311
- Fat: 16 g
- Saturated Fat: 4 g
- Carbohydrates: 23 g
- Fiber: 4 g
- Sodium: 149 mg
- Protein: 22 g

CHAPTER 2: VEGETARIAN AND VEGAN RECIPES

Broiled Lemon Pepper Sprouts

(Prepping time: 5-10 minutes\ Cooking time: 10 minutes |For 4 servings)

Ingredients

- Salt to taste
- 2 teaspoons lemon pepper seasoning
- 2 tablespoons olive oil
- 1 pound brussels sprouts, sliced

Directions

1. Take your Brussels and coat them with oil
2. Season the sprouts with salt and lemon pepper
3. Spread the prepared Brussels over the Cooking basket
4. Select the broil option, with the temperature set to 350 degrees F and timer set to 5 minutes
5. Let it cook, serve, and enjoy!

Nutrition Values (Per Serving)

- Calories: 229
- Fat: 18 g
- Saturated Fat: 2 g
- Carbohydrates: 12 g
- Fiber: 2 g
- Sodium: 441 mg
- Protein: 8 g

Baked Veggie Platter

(Prepping time: 5-10 minutes\ Cooking time: 25 minutes |For 4 servings)

Ingredients

- Olive oil as needed
- 18 ounces eggplant
- 4 garlic cloves
- 18 ounces zucchini
- Thyme sprig
- 18 ounces bell pepper
- Salt and pepper to taste
- 4 whole onions
- Bay leaf
- 18 ounces tomatoes
- Almond flour

Directions

1. Preheat your Fryer to 380 degrees F in "AIR FRY" mode
2. Cut tomatoes and bake them for 2 minutes
3. Mix eggplant with olive oil and spices, transfer to Air Fryer, and cook for 4 minutes
4. Cook zucchiniin your Air Fryer for 4 minutes (with olive oil)
5. Add tomatoes, bell pepper to the mix and bake for 2 minutes more (add more olive oil and almond flour if you prefer)
6. Serve and enjoy!

Nutrition Values (Per Serving)

- Calories: 279
- Fat: 10 g
- Saturated Fat: 2 g
- Carbohydrates: 13 g
- Fiber: 4 g
- Sodium: 245 mg
- Protein: 10 g

Basil And Tomato Meal

(Prepping time: 5-10 minutes\ Cooking time: 10 minutes |For 4 servings)

Ingredients

- 3 tomatoes, halved
- Olive oil
- Salt and pepper to taste
- 1 tablespoon fresh basil, chopped

Directions

1. Drizzle cut sides of the tomato halves with cooking spray evenly.
2. Sprinkle with salt, black pepper, and basil. Press "Power Button" of Air Fry Oven and turn the dial to select the "Air Fry" mode.
3. Press the Time button and again turn the dial to set the cooking time to 10 minutes.
4. Now push the Temp button and rotate the dial to set the temperature at 320 degrees F.
5. Press the "Start/Pause" button to start. When the unit beeps to show that it is preheated, open the lid.
6. Arrange the tomatoes in "Air Fry Basket" and insert them in the Oven. Serve warm.

Nutrition Values (Per Serving)

- Calories: 34
- Fat: 0.4 g
- Saturated Fat: 0.1 g
- Carbohydrates: 7 g
- Fiber: 2 g
- Sodium: 285 mg
- Protein: 1.7 g

Spinach And Carrot Platter

(Prepping time: 5-10 minutes\ Cooking time: 20 minutes |For 4 servings)

Ingredients

- Salt and pepper to taste
- 1 tablespoon fresh basil, chopped
- 1 pound zucchinis, sliced
- ¼ pound carrots, peeled and sliced
- 4 teaspoons butter, melted and divided

Directions

1. In a bowl, mix 2 teaspoons of the butter and carrots.
2. Press "Power Button" of Air Fry Oven and turn the dial to select the "Air Fry" mode.
3. Press the Time button and again turn the dial to set the cooking time to 35 minutes.
4. Now push the Temp button and rotate the dial to set the temperature at 400 degrees F.
5. Press the "Start/Pause" button to start.
6. When the unit beeps to show that it is preheated, open the lid.
7. Arrange the carrots in a greased "Air Fry Basket" and insert it in the Oven.
8. Meanwhile, in a large bowl, mix remaining butter, zucchini, basil, salt, and black pepper.
9. After 5 minutes of cooking, place the zucchini mixture into the basket with carrots.
10. Toss the vegetable mixture 2-3 times during the cooking.
11. Serve hot.

Nutrition Values (Per Serving)

- Calories: 64
- Fat: 4 g
- Saturated Fat: 2 g
- Carbohydrates: 6 g
- Fiber: 2 g
- Sodium: 1043 mg
- Protein: 2 g

Cauliflower And Broccoli Sauce

(Prepping time: 5-10 minutes\ Cooking time: 20 minutes |For 4 servings)

Ingredients

- 2/3 cup warm buffalo sauce
- 1 tablespoon butter, melted
- Salt and pepper to taste
- 2 teaspoons garlic powder
- 1 tablespoon olive oil
- 1 large head cauliflower, cut into bite-sized florets

Directions

1. In a large bowl, add cauliflower florets, olive oil, garlic powder, salt, pepper, and toss to coat.
2. Press "Power Button" of Air Fry Oven and select the "Air Fry" mode.
3. Press the Time button and again turn the dial to set the cooking time to 12 minutes.
4. Now push the Temp button and rotate the dial to set the temperature at 375 degrees F.
5. Press the "Start/Pause" button to start.
6. When the unit beeps to show that it is preheated, open the lid.
7. Arrange the cauliflower florets in "Air Fry Basket" and insert it in the Oven.
8. After 7 minutes of cooking, coat the cauliflower florets with buffalo sauce.
9. Serve hot.

Nutrition Values (Per Serving)

- Calories: 183
- Fat: 17 g
- Saturated Fat: 4 g
- Carbohydrates: 6 g
- Fiber: 2 g
- Sodium: 585 mg
- Protein: 2 g

Sweet And Sour Brussels

(Prepping time: 5-10 minutes\ Cooking time: 10 minutes |For 4 servings)

Ingredients

- Salt as needed
- ¼ teaspoon red pepper flakes, crushed
- 1 tablespoon maple syrup
- 1 tablespoon balsamic vinegar
- 2 cups brussels sprouts, trimmed and halved

Directions

1. In a bowl, add all the ingredients and toss to coat well.
2. Press the "Power Button" of the Air Fry Oven and select the "Air Fry" mode.
3. Press the Time button and again turn the dial to set the cooking time to 10 minutes.
4. Now push the Temp button and rotate the dial to set the temperature at 400 degrees F.
5. Press the "Start/Pause" button to start.
6. When the unit beeps to show that it is preheated, open the lid.
7. Arrange the Brussels sprouts in "Air Fry Basket" and insert it in the Oven.
8. Serve hot.

Nutrition Values (Per Serving)

- Calories: 66
- Fat: 0.4 g
- Saturated Fat: 0.1 g
- Carbohydrates: 14 g
- Fiber: 2 g
- Sodium: 350 mg
- Protein: 3 g

Mozzarella Eggplant Patties

(Prepping time: 5-10 minutes\ Cooking time: 2-5 minutes |For 4 servings)

Ingredients

- 1 can tomato sauce
- ½ cup milk
- 2 large eggs, beaten
- 2 tablespoons all-purpose flour
- 1 cup Monterey jack cheese, shredded
- 1 cup cheddar cheese, shredded
- 1 can jalapeno pepper

Directions

1. Preheat Air Fryer Pro Oven on the Bake function to 330 F.
2. Place the eggplant slices in a greased baking tray and cook for 6 minutes.
3. Take out the tray, top the eggplant with mozzarella cheese and cook for 30 more seconds—spread tomato sauce on one half of the bun.
4. Place the lettuce leaf on top of the sauce. Place the cheesy eggplant on top of the lettuce.
5. Top with onion rings and pickles and then with the other bun half to serve.

Nutrition Values (Per Serving)

- Calories: 562
- Fat: 25 g
- Saturated Fat: 10 g
- Carbohydrates: 52 g
- Fiber: 10 g
- Sodium: 538 mg
- Protein: 48 g

CHAPTER 3: CHICKEN AND POULTRY RECIPES

Elegant Soy Chicken

(Prepping time: 10 minutes\ Cooking time: 25 minutes| For 4 servings)

Ingredients

- 12 chicken thighs, skinless
- ½ cup of soy sauce
- 1 tablespoon cold water
- ½ cup white sugar
- ¼ cup apple cider vinegar
- 1 garlic clove, minced
- ½ teaspoon ginger, grounded
- 1 tablespoon cornstarch
- ¼ teaspoon pepper, grounded

Directions

1. Add all the listed ingredients in a mixing bowl except chicken
2. Mix them well
3. Season the chicken with salt and pepper
4. Grease your cooking pan with oil
5. Add chicken and soy sauce mixture on top
6. Preheat your Smart Oven Air Fryer Pro by pressing the "BAKE" mode at 350 degrees F
7. Set the timer for 25 minutes
8. Let it preheat until you hear a beep
9. Arrange the pan over the grill grate
10. Lock the lid and cook for 25 minutes
11. Serve and enjoy!

Nutrition Values (Per Serving)

- Calories: 570
- Fat: 5 g
- Saturated Fat: 2 g
- Carbohydrates: 23 g
- Fiber: 0 g
- Sodium: 819 mg
- Protein: 40 g

Herby Chicken Roast

(Prepping time: 5-10 minutes\ Cooking time: 5 hours| For 6 servings)

Ingredients

- 1 whole chicken
- 5 sprigs thyme, chopped
- 5 garlic cloves, crushed
- ¼ cup lemon juice
- 1 tablespoon canola oil
- ¼ cup honey
- 2 tablespoons salt
- 1 tablespoon pepper

Directions

1. Take the garlic cloves and push them into chicken cavities
2. Brush chicken with a mixture of lemon juice, honey, and oil on each and every sides
3. Season with thyme, salt, and pepper
4. Transfer to your Smart Oven Air Fryer Pro
5. Press the "ROAST" option and set it to 250 degrees F
6. Cook for 5 hours
7. Serve and enjoy!

Nutrition Values (Per Serving)

- Calories: 280
- Fat: 22 g
- Saturated Fat: 6 g
- Carbohydrates: 1 g
- Fiber: 0 g
- Sodium: 366 mg
- Protein: 19 g

Lemon And Mustard Roast Chicken

(Prepping time: 5-10 minutes\ Cooking time: 30 minutes |For 6 servings)

Ingredients

- 6 chicken thighs
- Salt and pepper to taste
- 3 teaspoons dried Italian seasoning
- 1 tablespoon oregano, dried
- ½ cup Dijon mustard
- ¼ cup of vegetable oil
- 2 tablespoons lemon juice

Directions

1. Take a bowl and add all listed ingredients except chicken
2. Mix everything well
3. Brush both sides of the chicken with the mixture, transfer chicken to the cooking basket
4. Set your Smart Oven Air Fryer Pro to roast mode, set temperature to 350 degrees F
5. Let it cook until the timer runs out
6. Serve and enjoy!

Nutrition Values (Per Serving)

- Calories: 797
- Fat: 52 g
- Saturated Fat: 20 g
- Carbohydrates: 45 g
- Fiber: 9 g
- Sodium: 1566 mg
- Protein: 42 g

Roasted Turkey Breast

(Prepping time: 5-10 minutes\ Cooking time: 10 minutes |For 6 servings)

Ingredients

- 3 pounds turkey breast, boneless
- ¼ cup mayonnaise
- 2 teaspoons poultry seasoning
- ¼ teaspoon pepper
- ½ teaspoon garlic powder
- 1 teaspoon salt

Directions

1. Whisk all the ingredients, including turkey, in a bowl, and coat it well.
2. Place the boneless turkey breast in the air fryer basket.
3. Select Air Fry mode
4. Press the Time button and again use the dial to set the cooking time to 50 minutes.
5. Now press the Temp button and rotate the dial to set the temperature at 350 degrees F.
6. Once preheated, place the air fryer basket in the Vortex Oven and Close its lid to bake.
7. Once done, slice and serve!

Nutrition Values (Per Serving)

- Calories: 222
- Fat: 11 g
- Saturated Fat: 3 g
- Carbohydrates: 14 g
- Fiber: 3 g
- Sodium: 779 mg
- Protein: 17 g

Blackened Chicken Meal

(Prepping time: 5-10 minutes\ Cooking time: 18 minutes |For 6 servings)

Ingredients

- 4 chicken breast
- 2 teaspoons olive oil

Seasoning

- 1 and ½ tablespoons brown sugar
- 1 teaspoon paprika
- 1 teaspoon dried oregano
- ¼ teaspoon garlic powder
- ½ teaspoon salt and pepper
- Chopped parsley for garnish

Directions

1. Mix olive oil with brown sugar, paprika, oregano, garlic powder, salt, and black pepper in a bowl.
2. Place the chicken breasts in the baking tray of the Air Fryer Oven
3. Pour and rub this mixture liberally over all the chicken breasts.
4. Select the "Bake" mode.
5. Hit the Time button and again use the dial to set the cooking time to 18 minutes.
6. Now push the Temp button and set the temperature at 425 degrees F.
7. Once preheated, place the baking tray inside the Oven. Serve warm.

Nutrition Values (Per Serving)

- Calories: 412
- Fat: 24 g
- Saturated Fat: 5 g
- Carbohydrates: 43 g
- Fiber: 9 g
- Sodium: 218 mg
- Protein: 18 g

Honey Flavored Chicken Drumstick

(Prepping time: 5-10 minutes\ Cooking time: 15 minutes |For 4 servings)

Ingredients

- 2 chicken drumstick, skin removed
- 2 teaspoons olive oil
- 2 teaspoons honey
- ½ teaspoon garlic, minced

Directions

1. Take a re-sealable zip bag and add olive oil, garlic, and honey; mix well
2. Add chicken to the bag and let it marinate for 30 minutes
3. Arrange drip pan in the bottom of the Air Fryer Oven cooking chamber
4. Preheat your Air Fryer to 300 degrees Fin "AIR FRY" mode
5. Transfer chicken to Air Fryer cooking basket and cook for 15 minutes
6. Serve and enjoy!

Nutrition Values (Per Serving)

- Calories: 797
- Fat: 52 g
- Saturated Fat: 24 g
- Carbohydrates: 45 g
- Fiber: 9 g
- Sodium: 144 mg
- Protein: 42 g

Excellent Chicken Tenders

(Prepping time: 5-10 minutes\ Cooking time: 10 minutes |For 6 servings)

Ingredients

- ½ cup fresh basil
- ¼ cup fresh cilantro
- 1 tablespoon olive oil
- 1 teaspoon garlic, minced
- 1 pound chicken fillet

Directions

1. Blend in fresh cilantro and basil in a blender
2. Add olive oil and minced garlic, stir well
3. Cut fillet into medium tenders and add basil mixture and stir
4. Arrange drip pan in the bottom of the Vortex Air Fryer Oven cooking chamber
5. Preheat your Fryer to 360 degrees F on "AIR FRY" mode
6. Add tenders to Air Fryer and cook for 9 minutes
7. Stir well
8. Once cooking is done, let them chill for and serve
9. Enjoy!

Nutrition Values (Per Serving)

- Calories: 250
- Fat: 26 g
- Saturated Fat: 5 g
- Carbohydrates: 3 g
- Fiber: 1 g
- Sodium: 436 mg
- Protein: 35 g

CHAPTER 4: FISH AND SEAFOOD RECIPES

Healthy Tuna Muffin

(Prepping time: 10 minutes\ Cooking time: 25 minutes |For 8 servings)

Ingredients

- 1 can tuna, flaked
- 1 and ½ cups cheddar cheese, shredded
- 2 eggs, lightly beaten
- ¼ cup mayonnaise
- 1 celery stalk, chopped
- ¼ cup sour cream
- 1 teaspoon cayenne pepper
- Salt and pepper

Directions

1. Take a large bowl and add all the ingredients to it
2. Mix them well
3. Pour into the greased muffin pan
4. Place the wire rack on Level 2
5. Preheat by pressing the "BAKE" option and setting it to 350 degrees F
6. Set the timer to 25 minutes
7. Let it preheat until you hear a beep
8. Place the baking dish on a wire rack and close the oven door
9. Cook for 25 minutes
10. Serve and enjoy!

Nutrition Values (Per Serving)

- Calories: 186
- Fat: 14 g
- Saturated Fat: 3 g
- Carbohydrates: 2.6 g
- Fiber: 1 g
- Sodium: 664 mg
- Protein: 13 g

Gently Baked Haddock

(Prepping time: 10 minutes\ Cooking time: 5-10 minutes |For 4 servings)

Ingredients

- ¼ teaspoon salt
- ¾ cup breadcrumbs
- ¼ cup parmesan cheese, grated
- ¼ teaspoon ground thyme
- ¼ cup butter, melted
- 1 pound haddock fillets
- ¾ cup milk

Directions

1. Take your fish fillets and dredge them well in milk, season with salt and keep them on the side
2. Take a medium-sized mixing bowl, add thyme
3. Add parmesan, cheese, breadcrumbs and mix well
4. Coat the fillets well with the crumb mixture
5. Set your Smart Oven Air Fryer Pro to BAKE
6. Set temperature to 325 degrees F, set the timer to 13 minutes
7. Transfer to the appliance, cook for 8 minutes
8. Flip and cook for 8 minutes more
9. Enjoy

Nutrition Values (Per Serving)

- Calories: 450
- Fat: 27 g
- Saturated Fat: 12 g
- Carbohydrates: 16 g
- Fiber: 22 g
- Sodium: 977 mg
- Protein: 44 g

Mango And Fish Salsa Meal

(Prepping time: 10 minutes\ Cooking time: 20 minutes| For 4 servings)

Ingredients

- 1 ripe mango
- 1 and ½ teaspoon red chili paste
- 3 tablespoons fresh coriander
- 1 lime juice
- 1 pound fish fillet
- 2 ounces shredded coconut

Directions

1. Peel the mango and cut it up into small cubes
2. Mix the mango cubes in a bowl alongside ½ a teaspoon of red chili paste, juice, zest of lime, and 1 tablespoon of coriander
3. Puree the fish in a food processor and mix with 1 teaspoon of salt and 1 egg
4. Add the rest of the lime zest, lime juice, and red chili paste
5. Mix well alongside the remaining coriander
6. Add 2 tablespoon of coconut and green onion
7. Put the rest of the coconut on a soup plate
8. Divide the fish mix into 12 portions and shape them into cakes
9. Coat with coconut
10. Arrange drip pan in the bottom of the Air Fryer Oven cooking chamber
11. Place six of the cakes in your Fryer and cook for 8 minutes until they are golden brown at 352-degree Fahrenheitin "AIR FRY" mode
12. Repeat until all cakes are used up
13. Serve with mango salsa
14. Enjoy!

Nutrition Values (Per Serving)

- Calories: 150
- Fat: 8 g
- Saturated Fat: 3 g
- Carbohydrates: 15 g
- Fiber: 4 g
- Sodium: 3084 mg
- Protein: 10 g

Hearty Flounder Delight

(Prepping time: 10 minutes\ Cooking time: 12 minutes| For 4 servings)

Ingredients

- 1 whole egg
- 1 cup dry breadcrumbs
- ¼ cup olive oil
- 3 (6 ounces each) flounder fillets
- 1 lemon, sliced

Directions

1. In a shallow bowl, beat the egg. In another bowl, add the breadcrumbs and oil and mix until a crumbly mixture is formed.
2. Dip flounder fillets into the beaten egg and then coat with the breadcrumb mixture.
3. Preheat Air Fry Oven and turn the select the "Air Fry" mode. Press the Time button and again turn the dial to set the cooking time to 12 minutes.
4. Now push the Temp button and rotate the dial to set the temperature at 356 degrees F. Press the "Start/Pause" button to start. When the unit beeps to show that it is preheated, open the lid.
5. Arrange the flounder fillets in a greased "Air Fry Basket" and insert it in the Oven.
6. Garnish with the lemon slices and serve hot.

Nutrition Values (Per Serving)

- Calories: 524
- Fat: 24 g
- Saturated Fat: 7 g
- Carbohydrates: 24 g
- Fiber: 9 g
- Sodium: 568 mg
- Protein: 24 g

Breaded Hake Dish

(Prepping time: 10 minutes\ Cooking time: 12 minutes/ For 4 servings)

Ingredients

- 1 whole egg
- 4 ounces breadcrumbs
- 2 tablespoons olive oil
- 4 (6 ounces) hake fillets
- 1 lemon, cut into wedges

Directions

1. In a shallow bowl, whisk the egg.
2. In another bowl, add the breadcrumbs and oil and mix until a crumbly mixture forms.
3. Dip fish fillets into the egg and then coat with the breadcrumbs mixture. Preheat Air Fryer Oven and select the "Air Fry" mode.
4. Press the Time button set the cooking time to 12 minutes.
5. Now push the Temp button and set the temperature at 350 degrees F.
6. Press the "Start/Pause" button to start. When the unit beeps to show that it is preheated, open the lid.
7. Arrange the hake fillets in a greased "Air Fry Basket" and insert it in the Oven.
8. Serve hot.

Nutrition Values (Per Serving)

- Calories: 297
- Fat: 10 g
- Saturated Fat: 3 g
- Carbohydrates: 22 g
- Fiber: 4 g
- Sodium: 1161 mg
- Protein: 29 g

Garlic Mussels

(Prepping time: 10 minutes\ Cooking time: 6 minutes| For 4 servings)

Ingredients

- 1 pound mussels
- 1 tablespoon butter
- 1 cup of water
- 2 teaspoons garlic, minced
- 1 teaspoon chives
- 1 teaspoon basil
- 1 teaspoon parsley

Directions

1. Toss the mussels with oil and all other ingredients in a bowl.
2. Spread the seasoned shrimp in the oven baking tray. Preheat Air Fry Oven and select the "Air Roast" mode.
3. Press the Time button and again turn the dial to set the cooking time to 6 minutes.
4. Now push the Temp button and rotate the dial to set the temperature at 390 degrees F.
5. Once preheated, place the mussel's tray in the Oven and close its lid.
6. Serve warm.

Nutrition Values (Per Serving)

- Calories: 125
- Fat: 6 g
- Saturated Fat: 4 g
- Carbohydrates: 5 g
- Fiber: 1 g
- Sodium: 500 mg
- Protein: 13 g

Mussels And Saffron Sauce

(Prepping time: 10 minutes\ Cooking time: 8 minutes| For 4 servings)

Ingredients

- 1 pound fresh mussels
- 4 threads saffron
- 3 tablespoons heavy cream
- ¼ cup dry white wine
- 1 tablespoon shallot, minced
- 1 tablespoon garlic, minced
- 1 tablespoon unsalted butter

Directions

1. Whisk cream with saffron, shallots, white wine, and butter in a bowl.
2. Place the mussels in the oven baking tray and pour the cream sauce on top.
3. Preheat Air Fryer Oven select the "Bake" mode.
4. Press the Time button and again turn the dial to set the cooking time to 8 minutes.
5. Now push the Temp button and rotate the dial to set the temperature at 370 degrees F.
6. Once preheated, place the mussel's baking tray in the Oven and close its lid. Serve warm.

Nutrition Values (Per Serving)

- Calories: 374
- Fat: 14 g
- Saturated Fat: 3 g
- Carbohydrates: 14 g
- Fiber: 3 g
- Sodium: 1450 mg
- Protein: 40 g

CHAPTER 5: BEEF AND LAMB RECIPES

Premium Onion Beef Roast

(Prepping time: 10 minutes\ Cooking time: 30 minutes |For 4 servings)

Ingredients

- Salt and pepper to taste
- 3 tablespoons olive oil
- 1 tablespoon butter
- Bunch of herbs
- 1 bulb garlic, peeled and crushed
- 2 sticks celery, sliced
- 2 medium onion, chopped
- 2 pounds topside beef

Directions

1. Take your mixing bowl, add the listed ingredients
2. Mix well
3. Set your Smart Oven Air Fryer Pro to in ROAST mode, set timer to 30 minutes
4. Transfer meat to cooking pan, let it cook until done
5. Serve and enjoy!

Nutrition Values (Per Serving)

- Calories: 320
- Fat: 17 g
- Saturated Fat: 4 g
- Carbohydrates: 11 g
- Fiber: 1.5 g
- Sodium: 293 mg
- Protein: 31 g

Tarragon Beef Shank

(Prepping time: 10 minutes\ Cooking time: 90 minutes |For 4 servings)

Ingredients

- 2 tablespoons olive oil
- 2 pounds beef shank
- Salt and pepper to taste
- 1 onion, diced
- 2 stalks celery, diced
- 1 cup Marsala wine
- 2 tablespoons dried tarragon

Directions

1. Place beef shanks in a baking pan, take a bowl and whisk in remaining ingredients
2. Pour over shanks
3. Place shanks in Air Fryer Basket
4. Arrange drip pan in the bottom of the Vortex Air Fryer Oven cooking chamber
5. Preheat your Air Fryer oven to 400 degrees F in "AIR FRY" mode
6. Set a timer to 90 minutes and cook at 400 degrees F
7. Once done, serve and enjoy

Nutrition Values (Per Serving)

- Calories: 320
- Fat: 17 g
- Saturated Fat: 3 g
- Carbohydrates: 11 g
- Fiber: 2 g
- Sodium: 185 mg
- Protein: 31 g

Bacon And Garlic Platter

(Prepping time: 10 minutes\ Cooking time: 30 minutes |For 4 servings)

Ingredients

- 4 potatoes, halved and peeled
- 6 garlic cloves, unpeeled and squashed
- 4 rashers streaky bacon, roughly cut
- 2 sprigs rosemary
- 1 tablespoon olive oil

Directions

1. Take a bowl and add garlic, bacon, rosemary, and potatoes
2. Add oil and mix well
3. Arrange drip pan in the bottom of the Air Fryer Oven cooking chamber
4. Preheat your Air Fryer to 392 degrees F in "AIR FRY" mode
5. Transfer mixture to Air Fryer cooking basket and roast for 25-30 minutes
6. Serve and enjoy!

Nutrition Values (Per Serving)

- Calories: 240
- Fat: 14 g
- Saturated Fat: 4 g
- Carbohydrates: 32 g
- Fiber: 3 g
- Sodium: 636 mg
- Protein: 6 g

Jerk Lamb Kebob

(Prepping time: 10 minutes\ Cooking time: 18 minutes |For 4 servings)

Ingredients

- A handful of thyme leaves, chopped
- 1 tablespoon honey
- 1 lime, zest, and juice
- 2 tablespoon jerk paste
- 2 pounds lamb steak

Directions

1. Mix lamb with jerk paste, lime juice, zest, honey, and thyme.
2. Toss well to coat, then marinate for 30 minutes.
3. Alternatively, thread the lamb on the skewers.
4. Place these lamb skewers in the Air fry basket.
5. Preheat Air Fry Oven and select the "Air fryer" mode.
6. Press the Time button set the cooking time to 18 minutes.
7. Now push the Temp button set the temperature at 360 degrees F.
8. Once preheated, place the Air fryer basket in the Oven and close its lid.
9. Flip the skewers when cooked halfway through, then resume cooking. Once ready, serve, and enjoy!

Nutrition Values (Per Serving)

- Calories: 548
- Fat: 22 g
- Saturated Fat: 6 g
- Carbohydrates: 17 g
- Fiber: 3 g
- Sodium: 319 mg
- Protein: 40 g

CHAPTER 6:SNACKS AND APPETIZERS

Cool Italian Egg Muffin

(Prepping time: 10 minutes\ Cooking time: 20 minutes |For 12 servings)

Ingredients

- 8 eggs
- 1/3 cup feta cheese, crumbled
- ½ cup tomatoes, sliced and sun-dried
- 5 basil leaves, chopped
- ½ onion, diced
- 1 cup spinach, diced
- ¼ cup milk
- Salt and pepper

Directions

1. Take your muffin pan and divide spinach, tomatoes, feta cheese, and onion into it
2. Add whisked eggs with milk, basil, salt, and pepper into a bowl
3. Pour egg mixture over vegetable mixture
4. Place the wire rack on Level 2
5. Preheat by pressing the "BAKE" option and setting it to 350 degrees F
6. Set the timer to 20 minutes
7. Let it preheat until you hear a beep
8. Place the baking dish on a wire rack and close the oven door
9. Cook for 20 minutes
10. Serve and enjoy!

Nutrition Values (Per Serving)

- Calories: 55
- Fat: 4 g
- Saturated Fat: 2 g
- Carbohydrates: 1.3 g
- Fiber: 1 g
- Sodium: 232 mg
- Protein: 5 g

Zucchini Cheesy Muffins

(Prepping time: 10 minutes\ Cooking time: 25 minutes |For 4 servings)

Ingredients

- 2 cups zucchini, shredded
- ½ cup feta cheese, crumbled
- ¼ cup onion, diced
- 1 egg, lightly beaten
- Salt and pepper

Directions

1. Take a large bowl and all the ingredients
2. Mix them well
3. Pour into the greased muffin pan
4. Place the wire rack on Level 2
5. Preheat by pressing the "BAKE" option and setting it to 350 degrees F
6. Set the timer to 25 minutes
7. Let it preheat until you hear a beep
8. Place the baking dish on a wire rack and close the oven door
9. Cook for 25 minutes
10. Serve and enjoy!

Nutrition Values (Per Serving)

- Calories: 80
- Fat: 5.3 g
- Saturated Fat: 2 g
- Carbohydrates: 3.5 g
- Fiber: 1 g
- Sodium: 172 mg
- Protein: 5 g

The Mexican Hash Browns

(Prepping time: 15 minutes\ Cooking time: 30 minutes |For 4 servings)

Ingredients

- 11 ounces baby potatoes
- 2 tablespoons sour cream, low-fat
- 2 cut bacon slices
- 1 teaspoon olive oil
- 1 and ½ ounces cheddar cheese, low-fat and shredded

Directions

1. Soak the potatoes in water
2. Preheat your Air fryer to 320 degrees F
3. Use a towel to drain and dry the potatoes
4. Drizzle some olive oil over the potatoes
5. Coat them well
6. Transfer to the air frying basket
7. Add jalapeno, onion, and bell pepper
8. Sprinkle half teaspoon olive oil, salt, and pepper
9. Transfer potatoes with a veg mix from Fryer
10. Place empty basket and raise the temperature to 356 degrees F
11. Toss the contents of your bowl
12. Cook for 30 minutes
13. Cook until the potatoes become crispy and brown
14. Serve and enjoy!

Nutrition Values (Per Serving)

- Calories: 197
- Fat: 5 g
- Saturated Fat: 2 g
- Carbohydrates: 34 g
- Fiber: 5 g
- Sodium: 644 mg
- Protein: 4 g

Brownie And Caramel Sauce

(Prepping time: 10 minutes\ Cooking time: 10-20 minutes| For 4 servings)

Ingredients

- 4 ounces caster sugar
- 2 tablespoons water
- ½ cup milk
- 4 ounces butter
- 2 ounces chocolate
- 6 ounces brown sugar
- 2 thoroughly beaten eggs
- 2 teaspoons vanilla essence

Directions

1. Preheat your Air Fryer to 356 degrees F in "AIR FRY" mode
2. Take a bowl and add butter, chocolate
3. Pour mixture into the pan and place it over medium heat
4. Take a bowl and add beaten eggs, sugar, vanilla essence, raising flour, and mix well
5. Take a dish and grease it
6. Pour beaten egg mixture into the dish
7. Transfer dish to the Air Fryer cooking basket and cook for 15 minutes
8. Take another pan and add caster sugar, heat until melted
9. Stir in butter into the caramel and let it melt
10. Top brownies with caramel and enjoy!

Nutrition Values (Per Serving)

- Calories: 250
- Fat: 12 g
- Saturated Fat: 2 g
- Carbohydrates: 30 g
- Fiber: 10 g
- Sodium: 840 mg
- Protein: 3 g

Awesome Lava Cake

(Prepping time: 10 minutes\ Cooking time: 5 minutes| For 4 servings)

Ingredients

- 3 ½ oz butter, melted
- 3 ½ tbsp sugar
- 1 ½ tbsp self-rising flour
- 3 ½ oz dark chocolate, melted
- 2 eggs

Directions

1. Grease 4 ramekins with butter. Preheat Air Fryer Smart Oven on Bake function to 375 F.
2. Beat the eggs and sugar until frothy. Stir in butter and chocolate; gently fold in the flour.
3. Divide the mixture between the ramekins and bake for 10 minutes.
4. Let cool for 2 minutes before turning the cakes upside down onto serving plates.

Nutrition Values (Per Serving)

- Calories: 703
- Fat: 48 g
- Saturated Fat: 10 g
- Carbohydrates: 61 g
- Fiber: 10 g
- Sodium: 73 mg
- Protein: 10 g

Sesame Banana Snack

(Prepping time: 10 minutes\ Cooking time: 8-10 minutes| For 4 servings)

Ingredients

- ½ tablespoon sugar
- 1 teaspoon baking powder
- 2 whole eggs, beaten
- 1 cup of water
- 3 tablespoon sesame seeds
- 1 teaspoon salt
- 5 bananas, sliced
- 1 and ½ cup flour

Directions

1.   Preheat Air Fryer Smart Oven
Pro on Bake function to 340 F. In a bowl, mix salt, sesame seeds, flour, baking powder, eggs, sugar, and water.
2.   Coat sliced bananas with the flour mixture. Place the prepared slices in the Air Fryer tray and fit in the baking tray;
3.   cook for 8-10 minutes. Serve chilled.

Nutrition Values (Per Serving)

- Calories: 425
- Fat: 20 g
- Saturated Fat: 8 g
- Carbohydrates: 59 g
- Fiber: 4 g
- Sodium: 237 mg
- Protein: 9 g

Vanilla And Almond Cookies

(Prepping time: 10 minutes\ Cooking time: 14 minutes| For 4 servings)

Ingredients

- Melted dark chocolate, to drizzle
- 1 and ½ teaspoon vanilla
- 2 teaspoons lemon juice
- 1 and 1/3 cups sugar
- ½ teaspoon almond extract
- 8 egg whites

Directions

1. In a bowl, add egg whites and lemon juice. Beat using an electric mixer until foamy. Slowly add the sugar and continue beating until thoroughly combined;
2. stir in almond and vanilla extracts.
3. Line the Air Fryer pan with parchment paper. Fill a piping bag with the meringue mixture and pipe as many mounds on the baking pan as you can, leaving 2-inch spaces between each mound.
4. Cook at 350 F for 5 minutes on the Bake function.
5. Reduce the temperature to 320 F and bake for 15 more minutes.
6. Then, reduce the heat to 190 F and cook for 15 minutes.
7. Let cool for 2 hours. Drizzle with dark chocolate and serve

Nutrition Values (Per Serving)

- Calories: 308
- Fat: 21 g
- Saturated Fat: 4 g
- Carbohydrates: 26 g
- Fiber: 8 g
- Sodium: 25 mg
- Protein: 4 g

Printed in the USA
CPSIA information can be obtained
at www.ICGtesting.com
LVHW080746140124
768651LV00014B/1195